Vintage Deer Coloring Book for Adults

Relaxation with Deer Coloring Pages of Realistic Hand-Drawn Illustrations

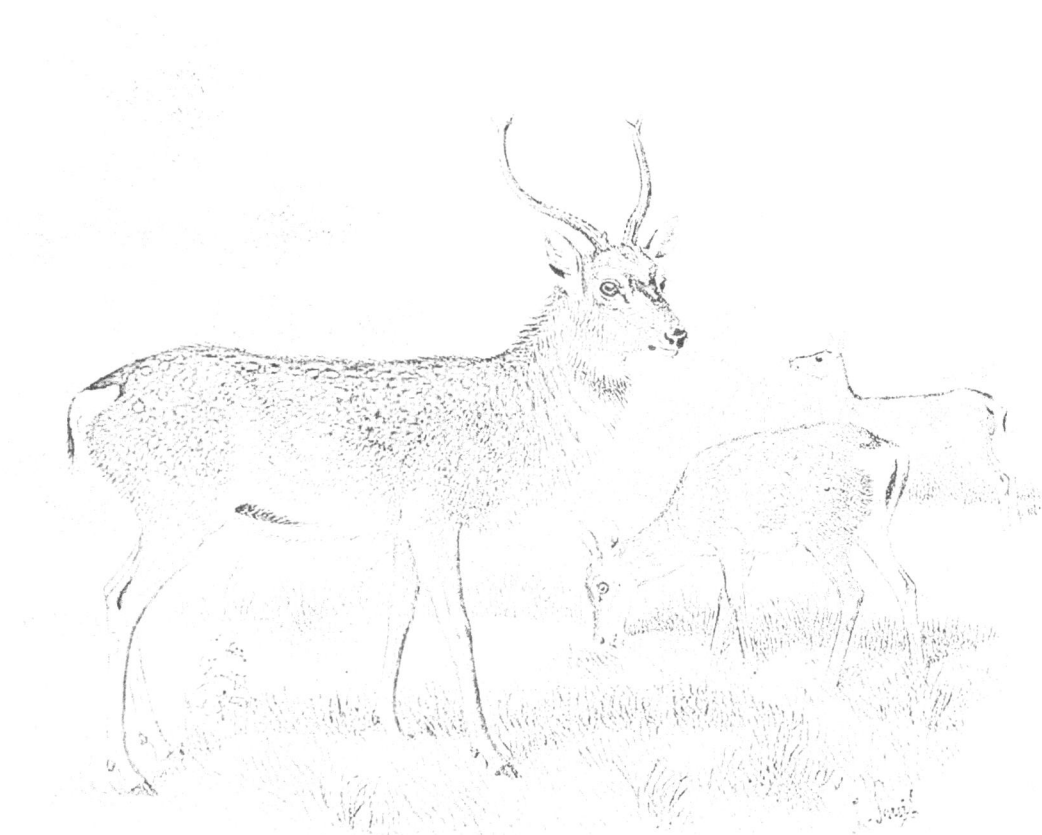

Ada Ashley

©LeVintagePrintage

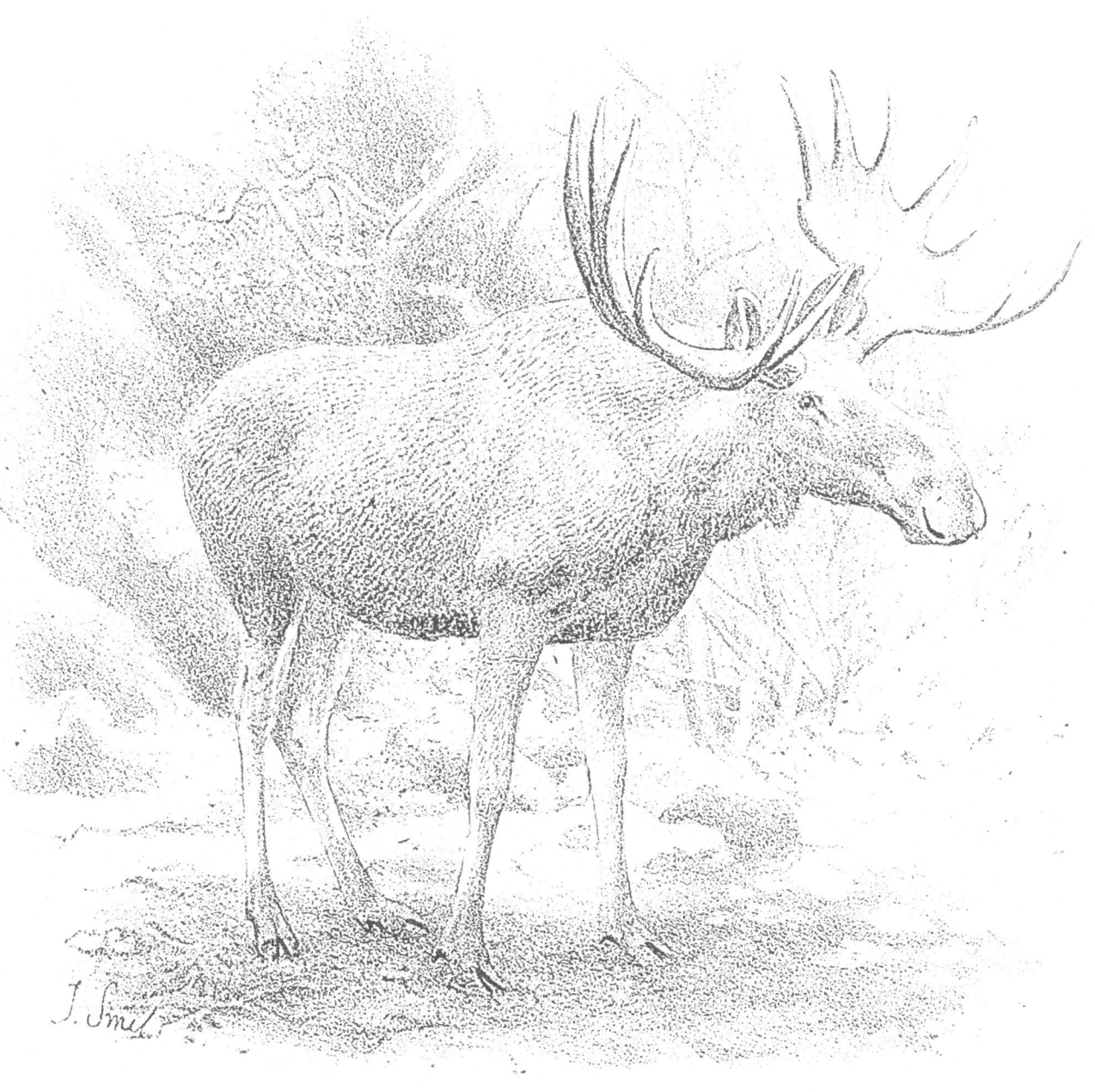

MALE ELK.

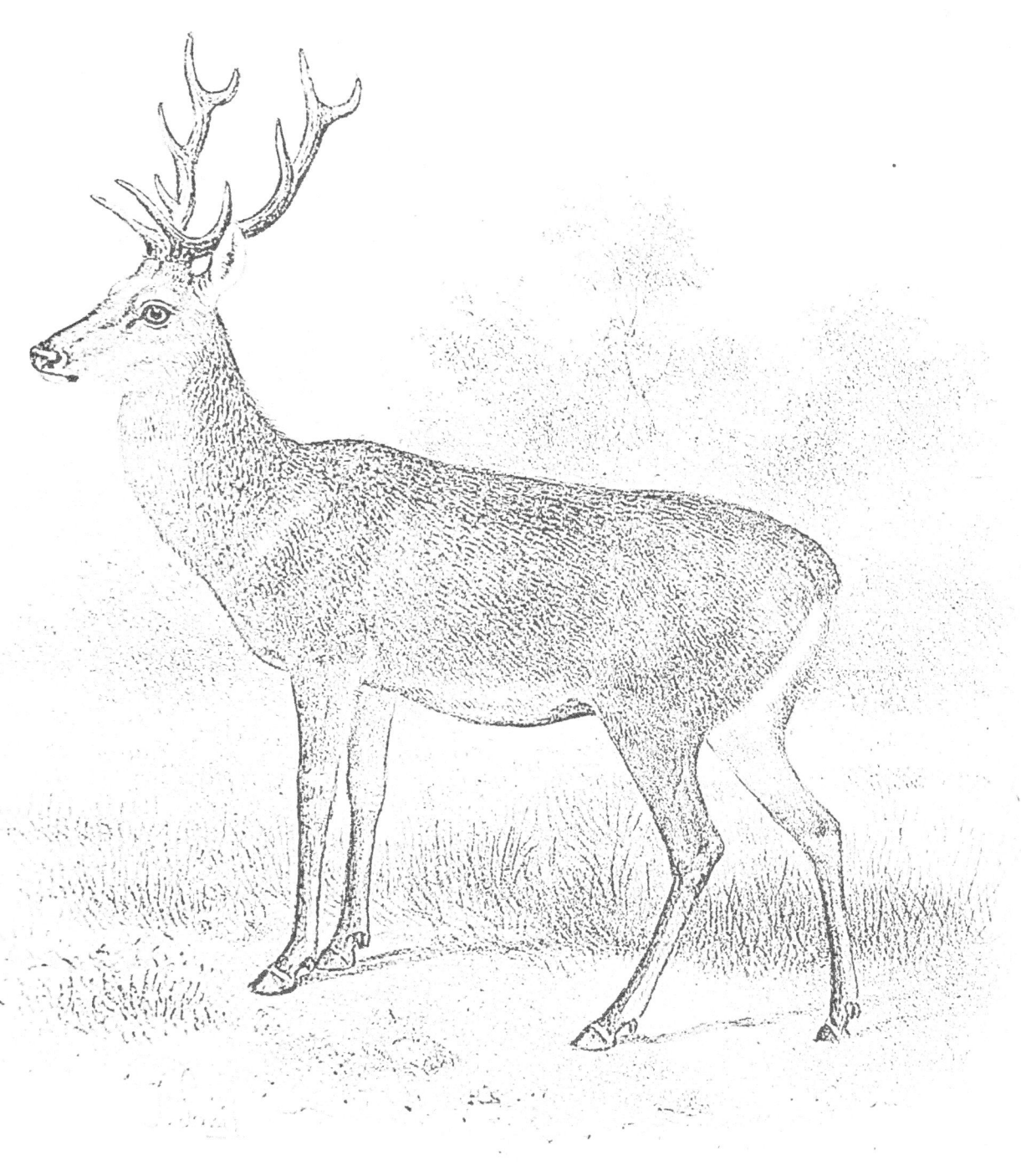

BEDFORD'S DEER IN SUMMER PELAGE.

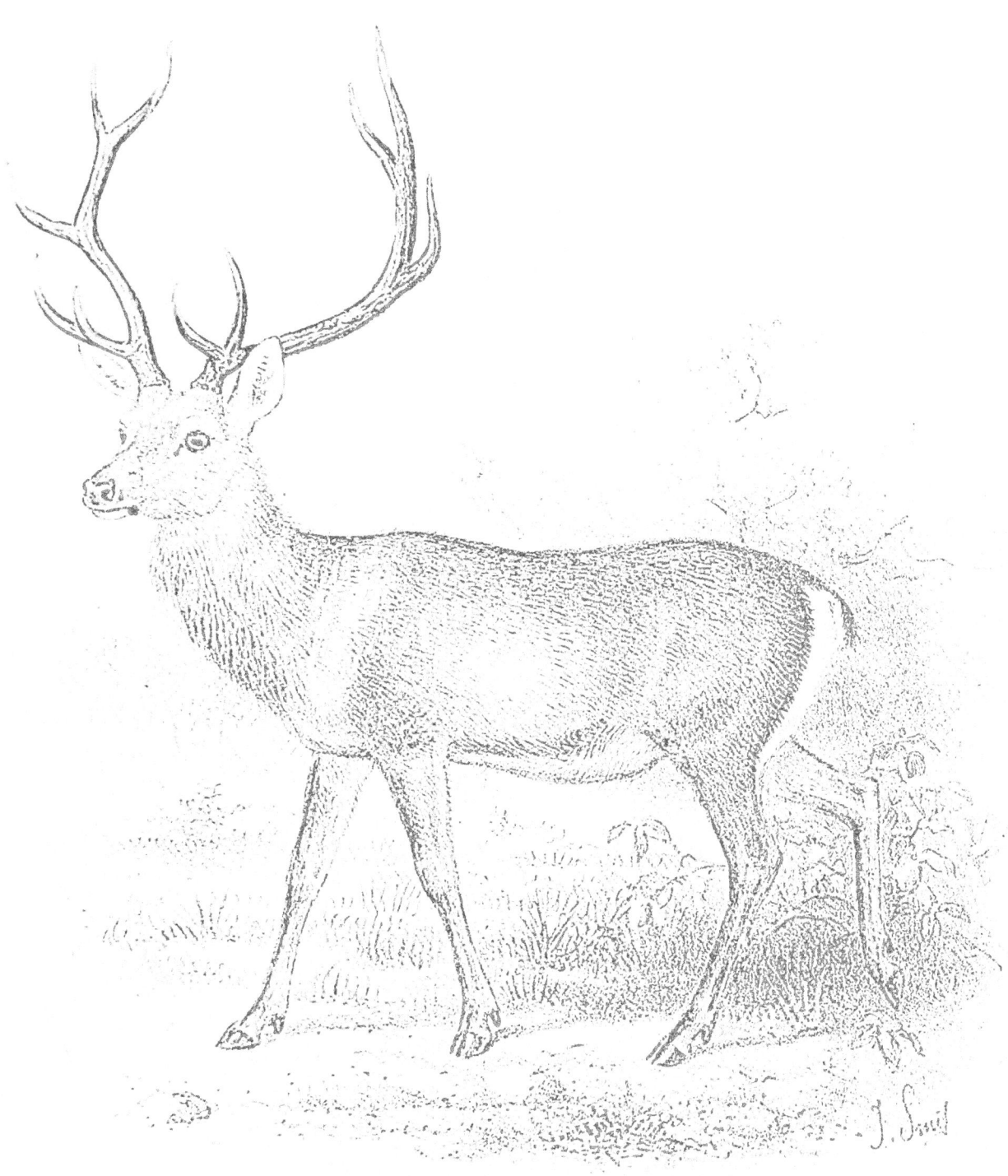

HANGUL.

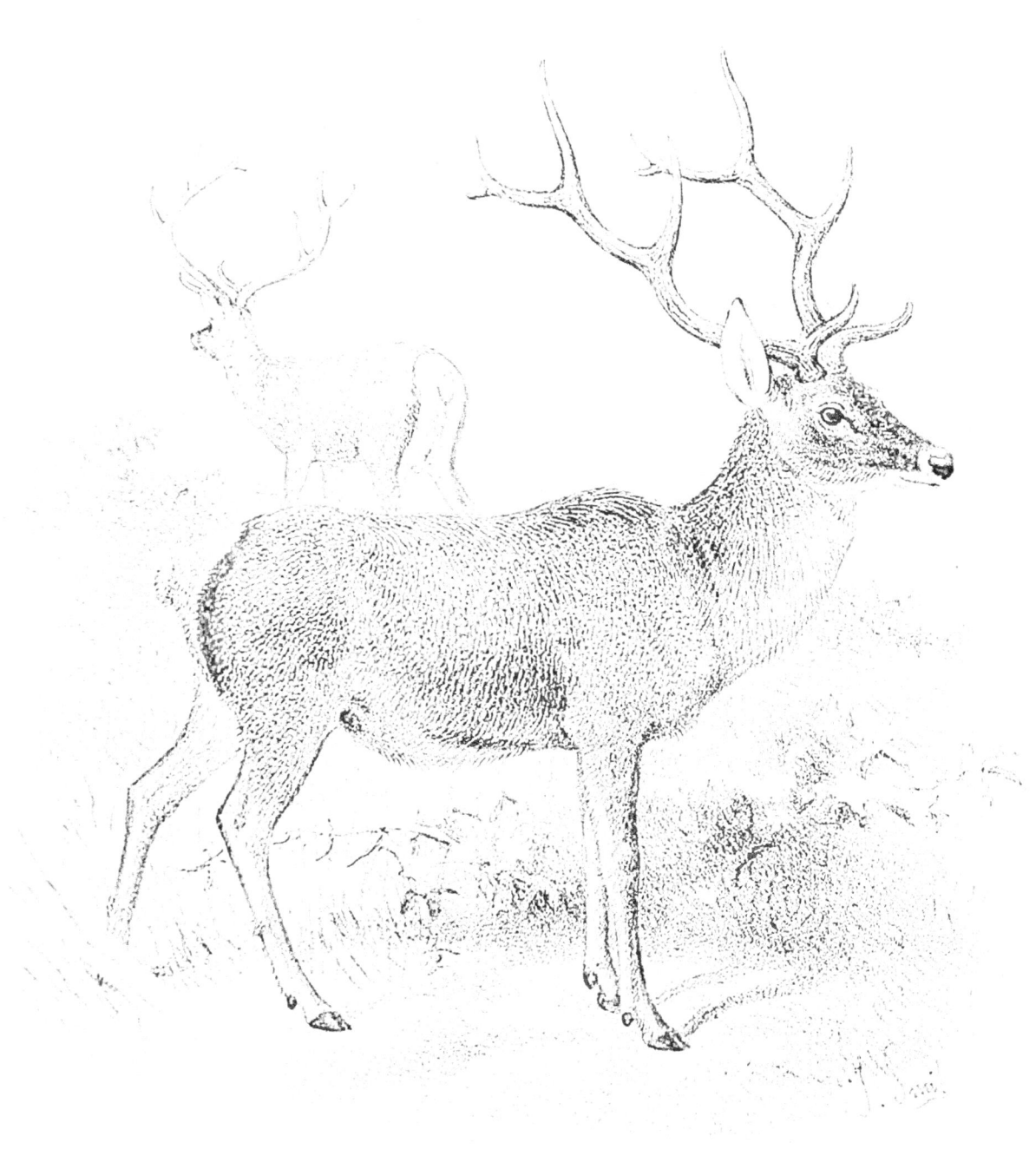

THOROLD'S DEER.

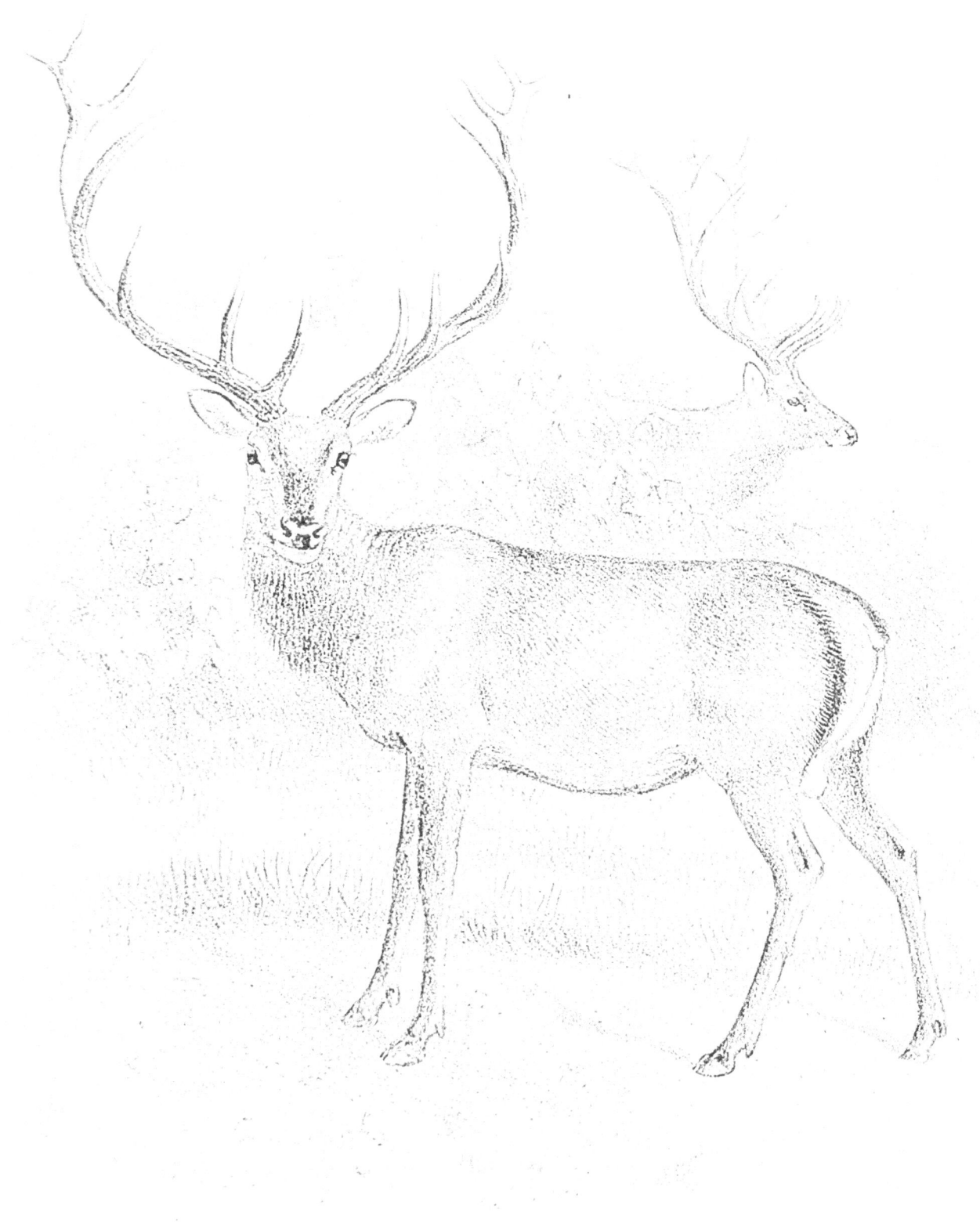

ALTAI WAPITI.

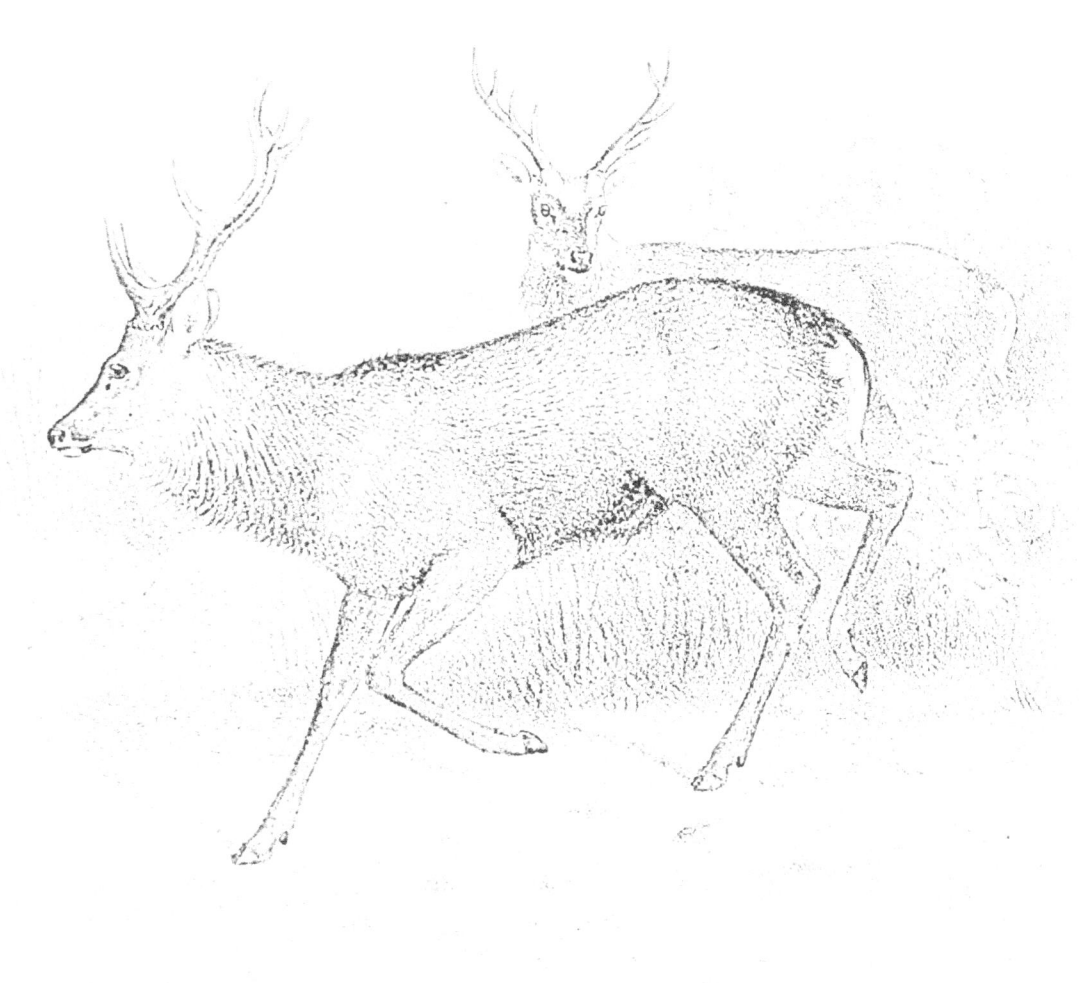

MANCHURIAN SIKA IN WINTER PELAGE.

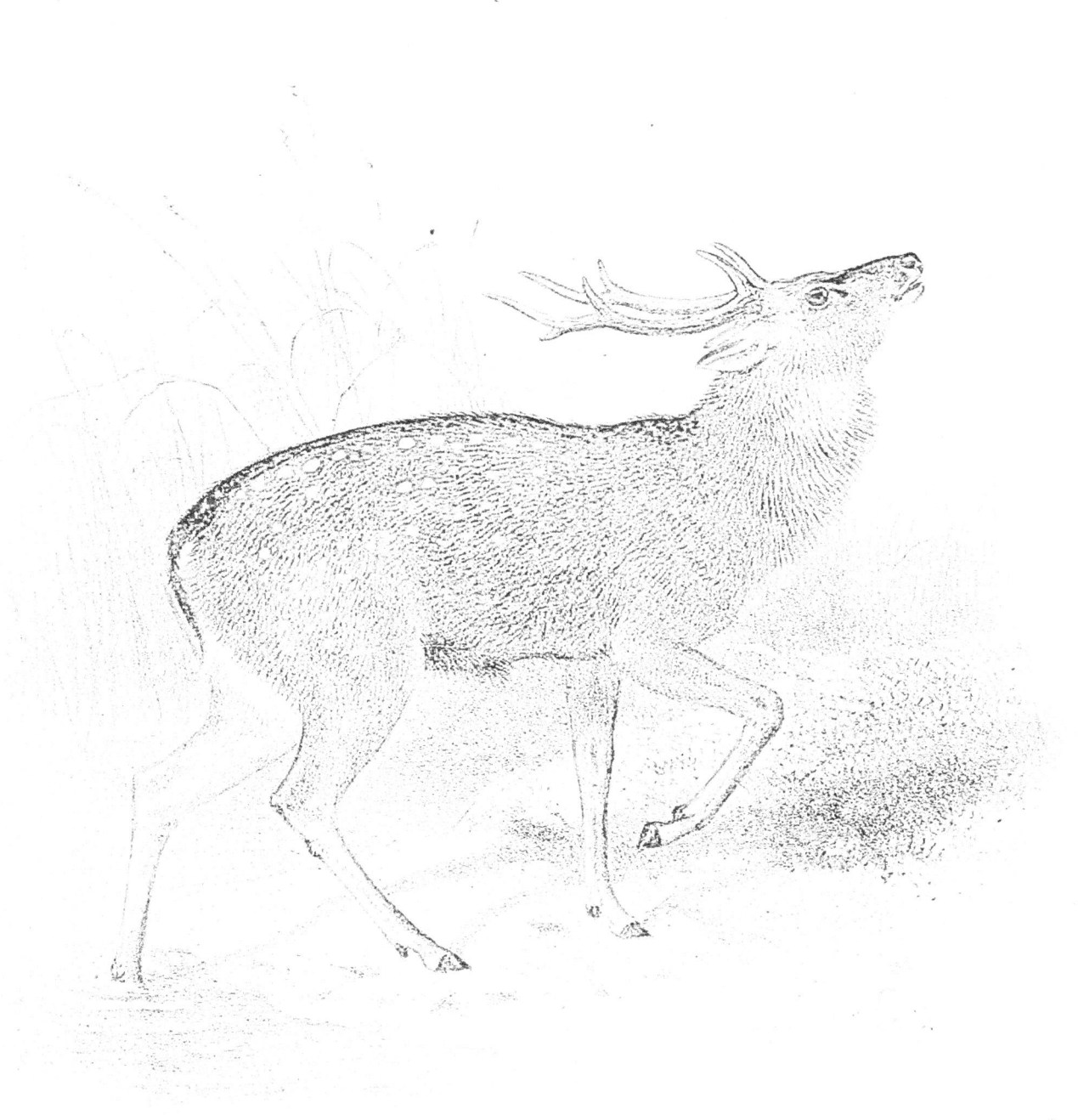

FORMOSAN SIKA IN WINTER PELAGE.

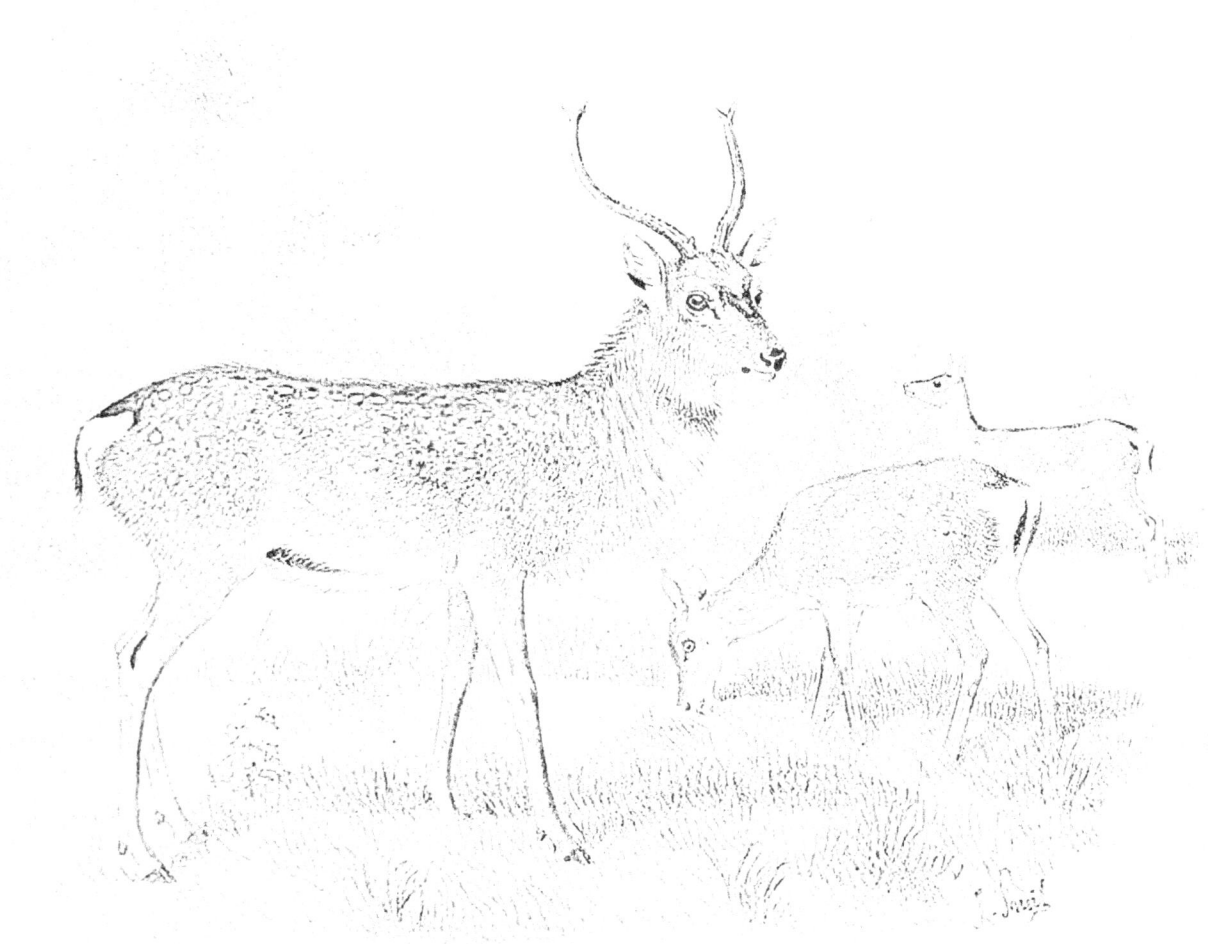

PEKIN SIKA IN WINTER PELAGE.

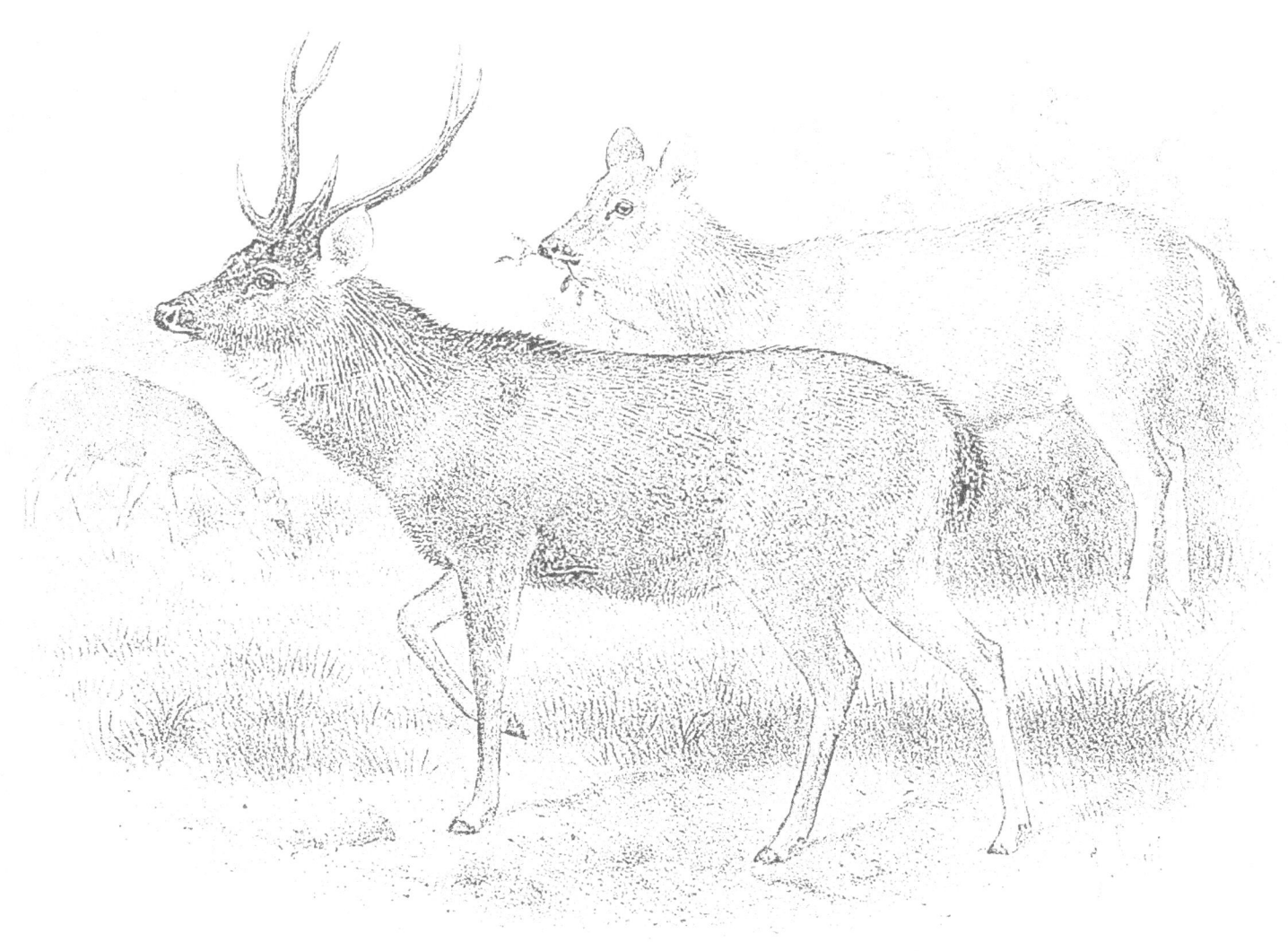

INDIAN SAMBAR, STAG AND HIND.

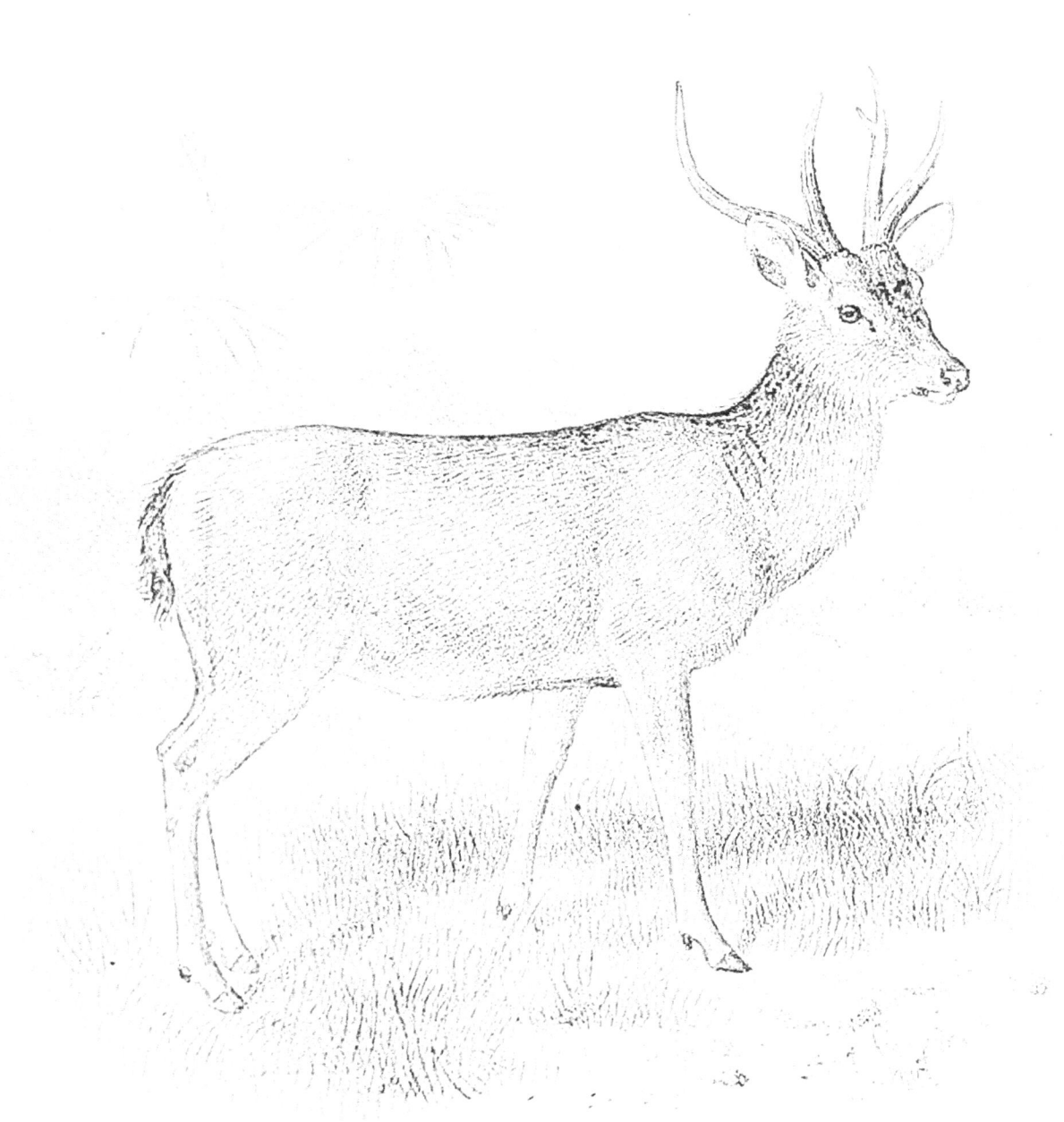

MALAYAN SAMBAR.

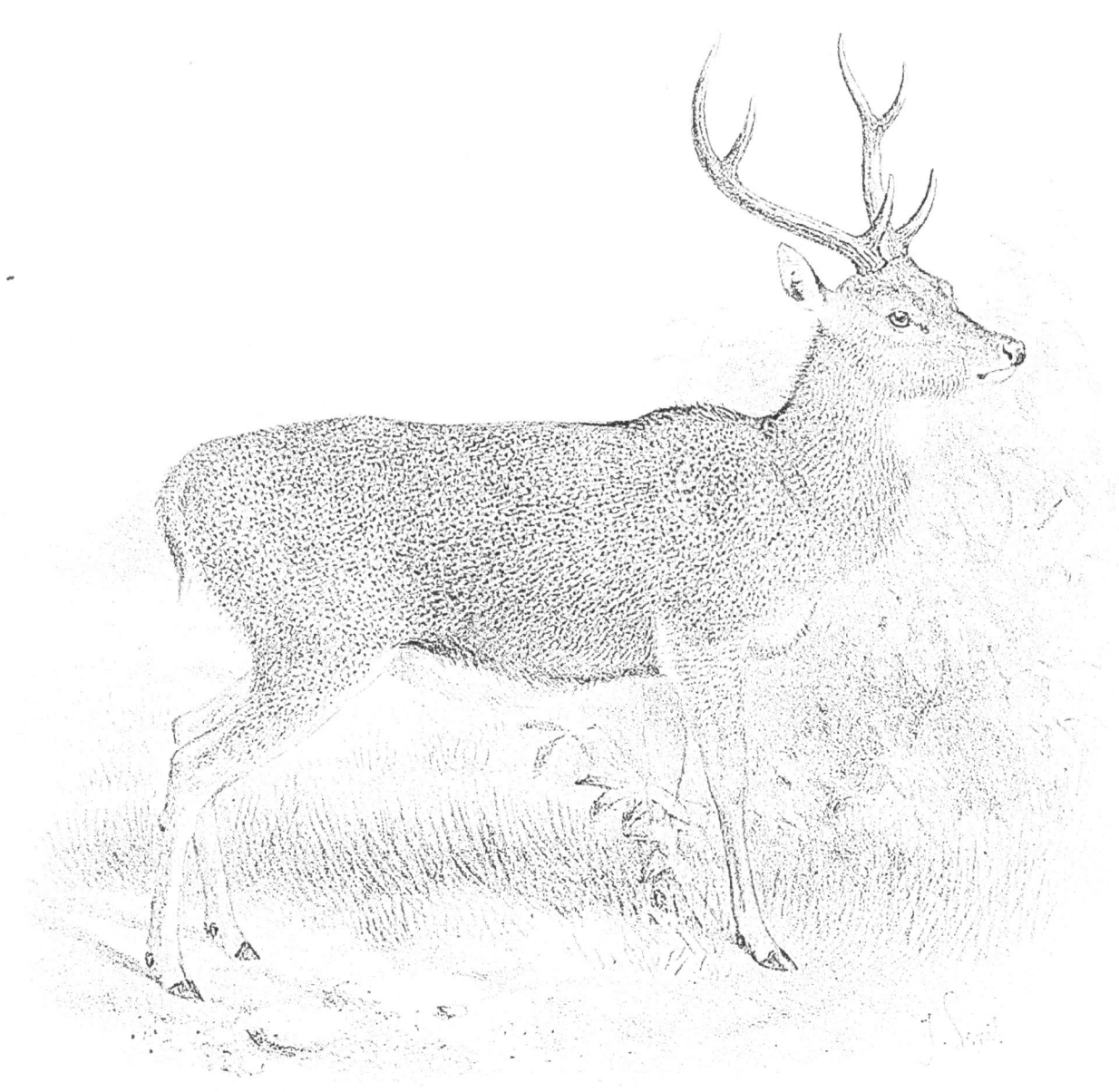

MOLUCCAN RUSA.

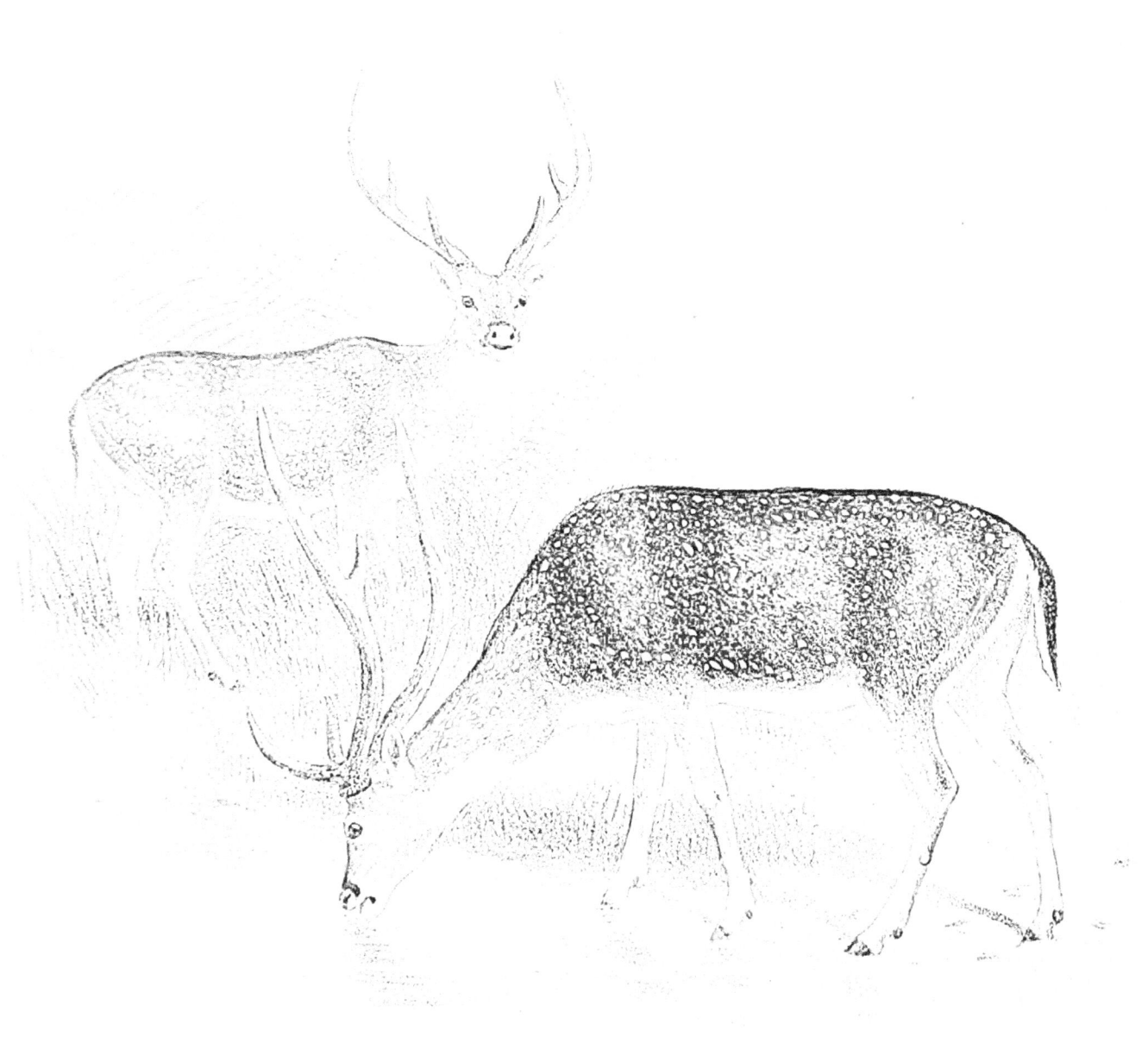

CHITAL, OR, INDIAN SPOTTED DEER.

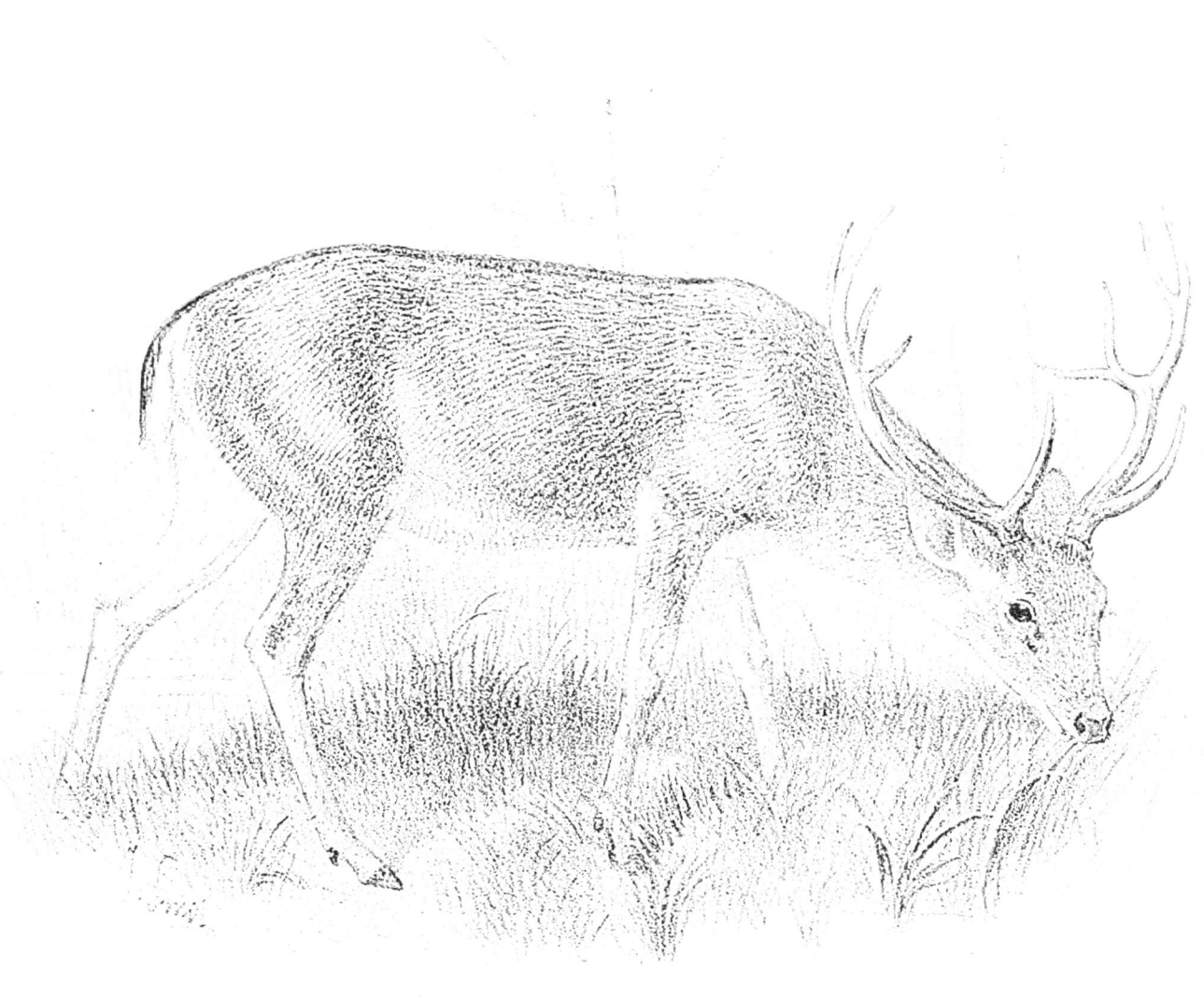

SWAMP-DEER.

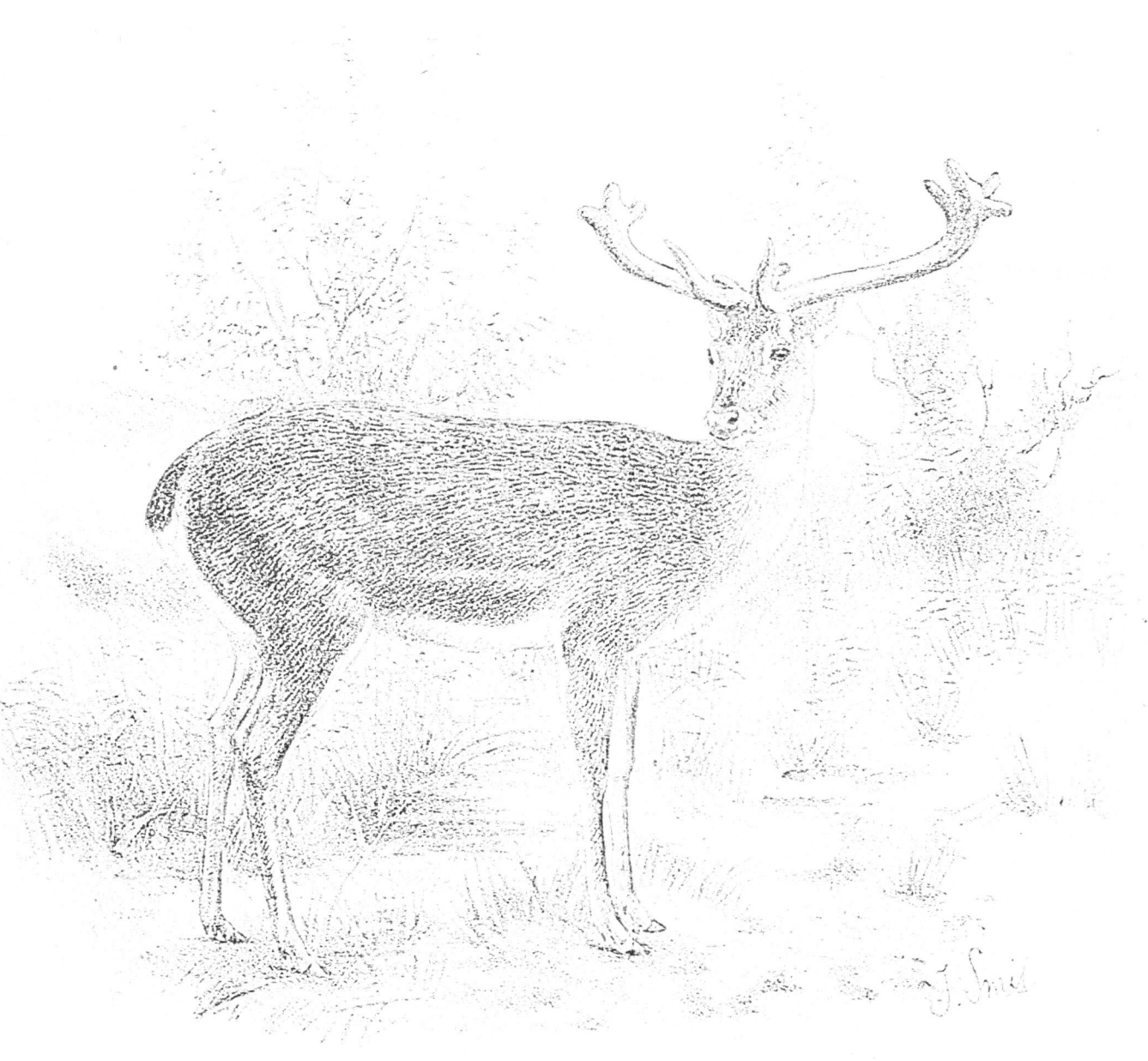

SIAMESE THAMENG IN WINTER PELAGE.

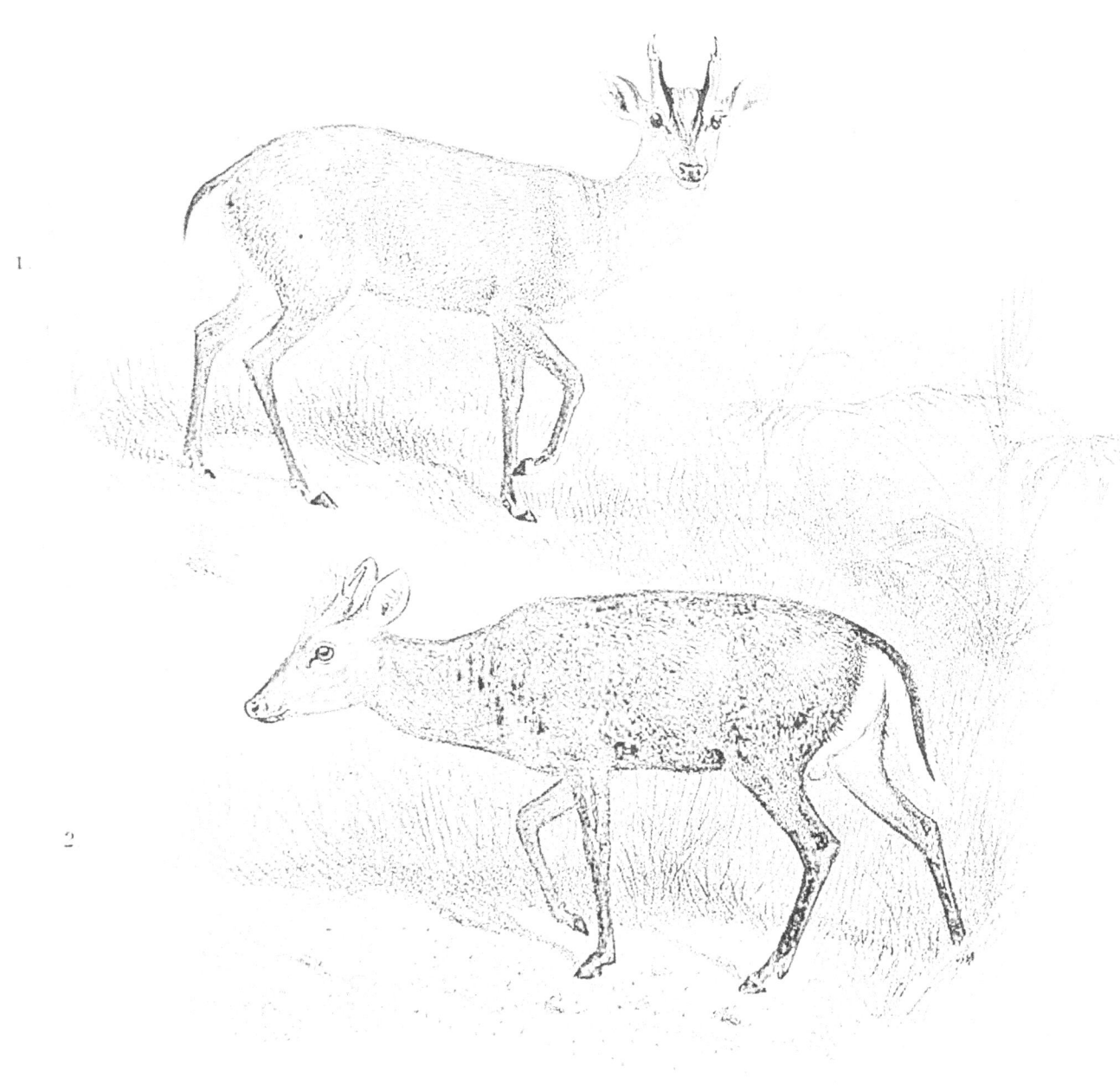

TENASSERIM (1) AND HAIRY-FRONTED (2) MUNTJACS.

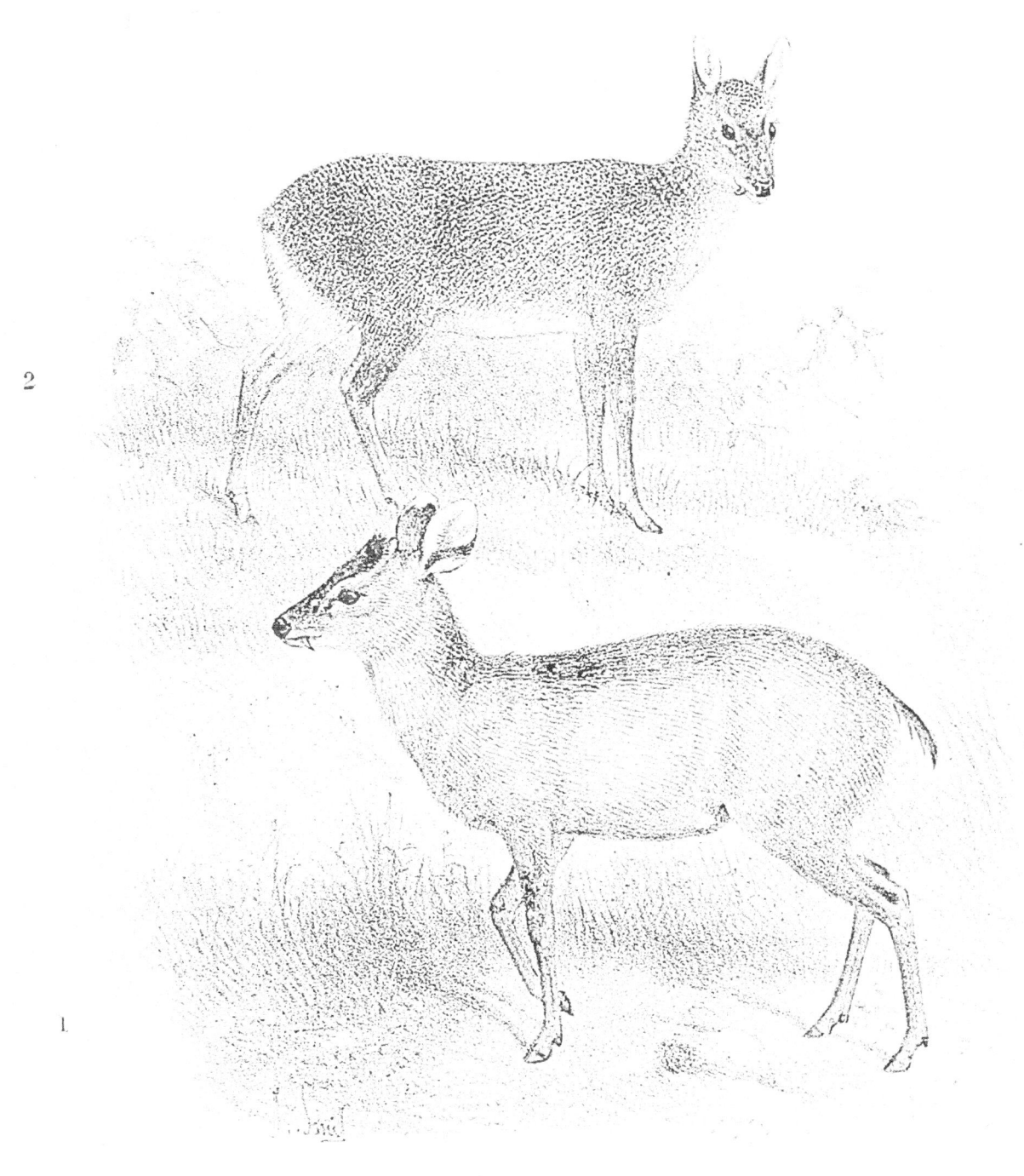

MICHIE'S TUFTED DEER (1) AND CHINESE WATER-DEER (2).

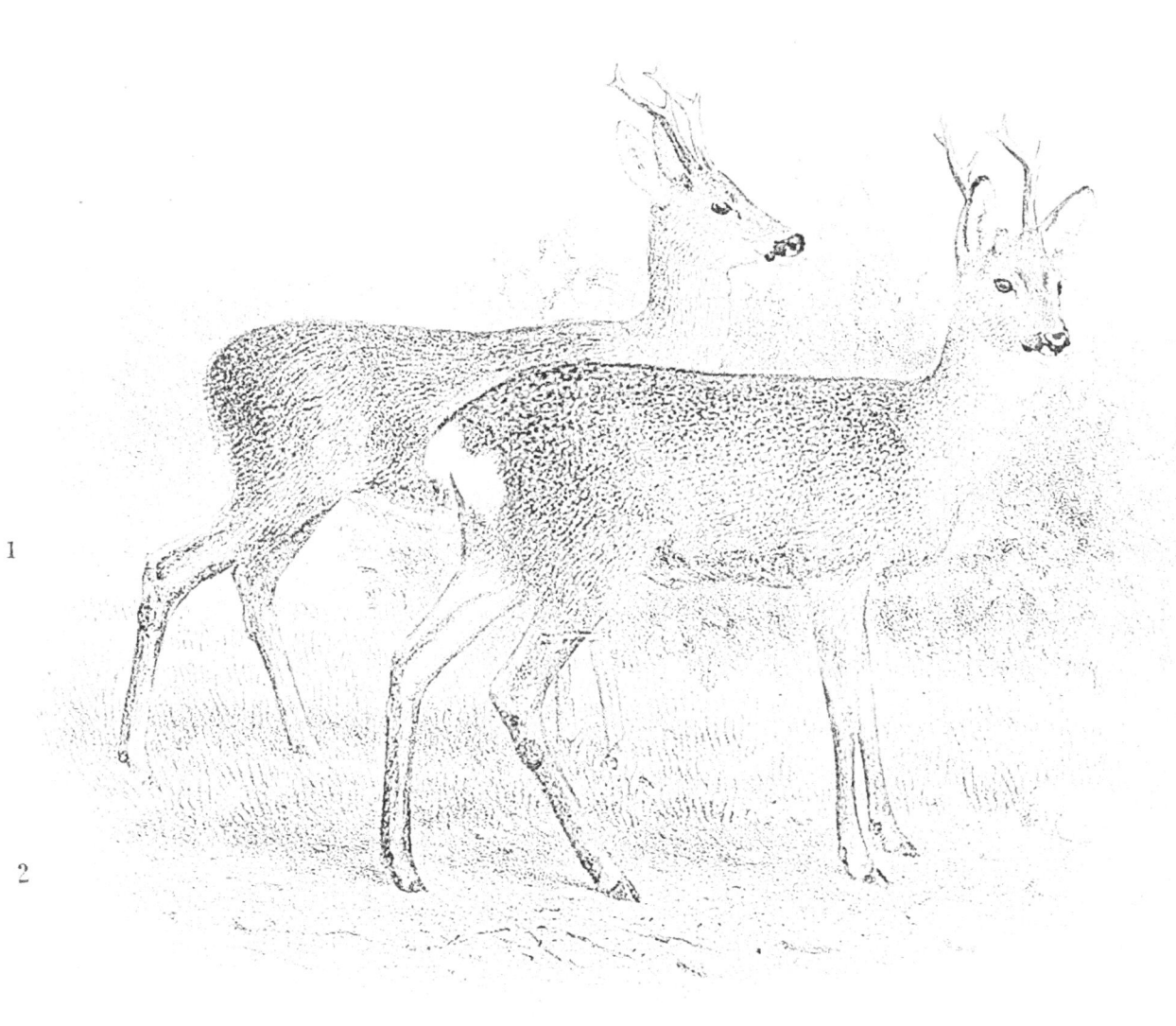

1

2

EUROPEAN ROE IN SUMMER (1) AND WINTER (2) PELAGE.

PÈRE DAVID'S DEER.

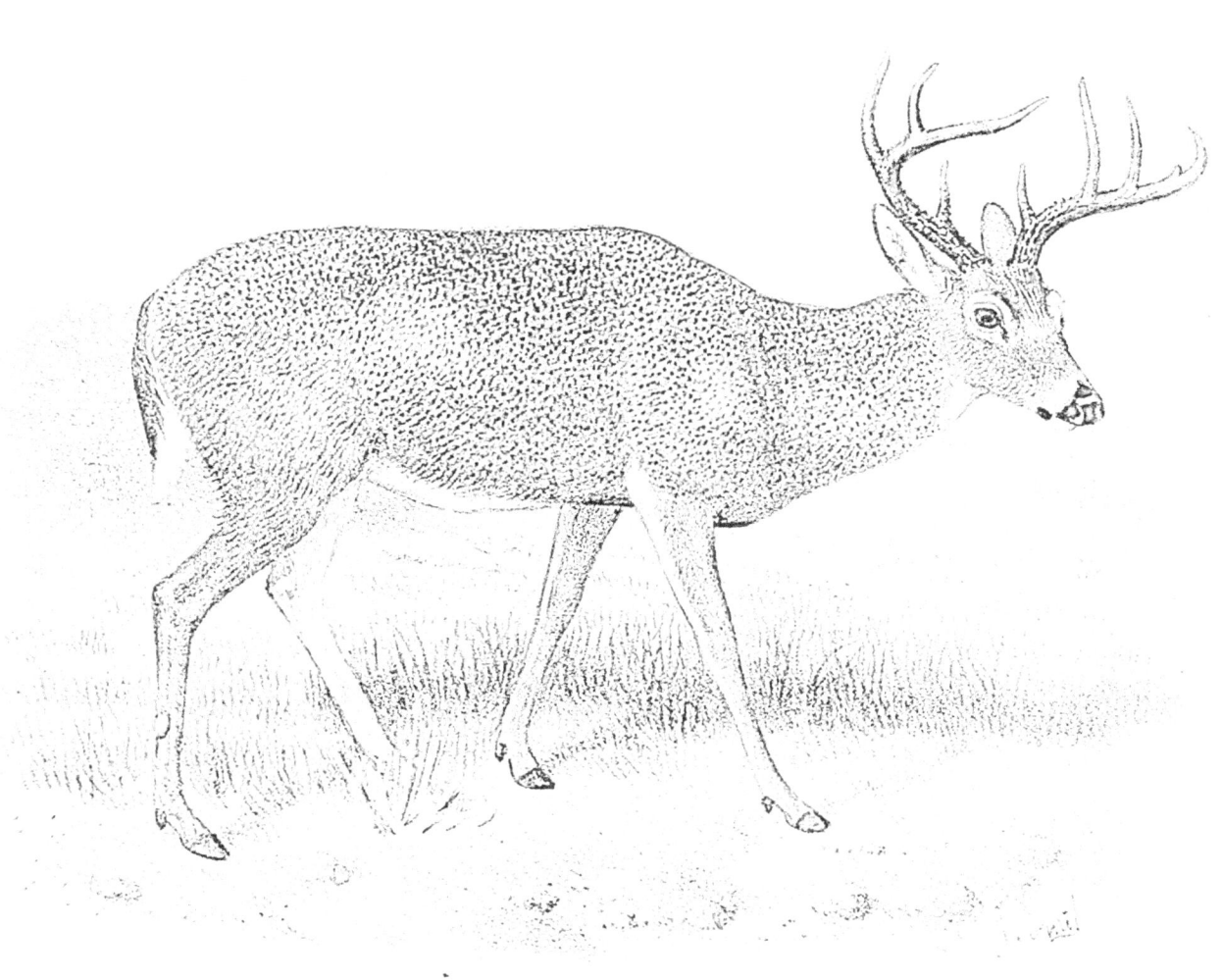

VIRGINIAN DEER IN WINTER PELAGE.

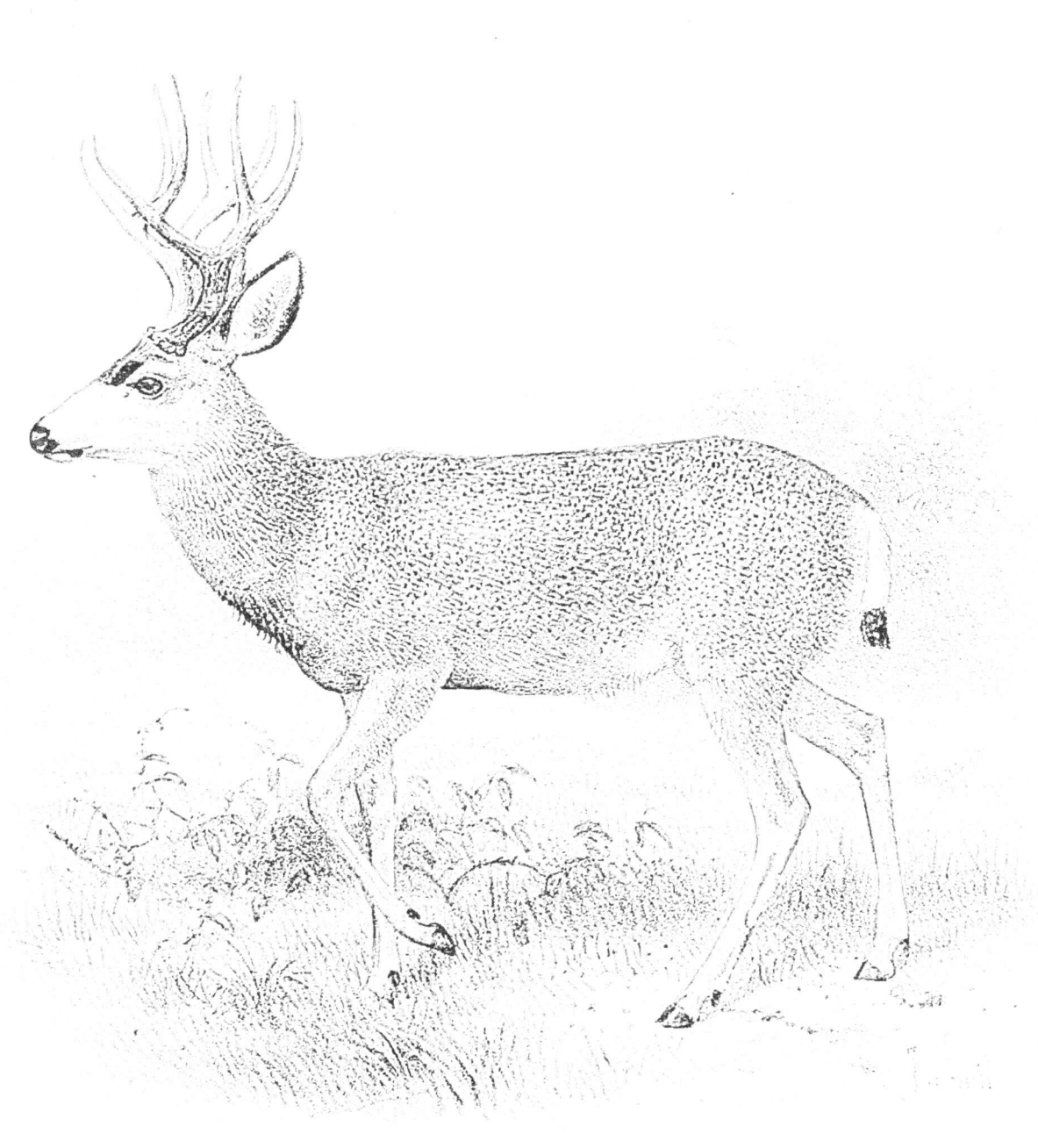

MULE-DEER IN WINTER PELAGE.

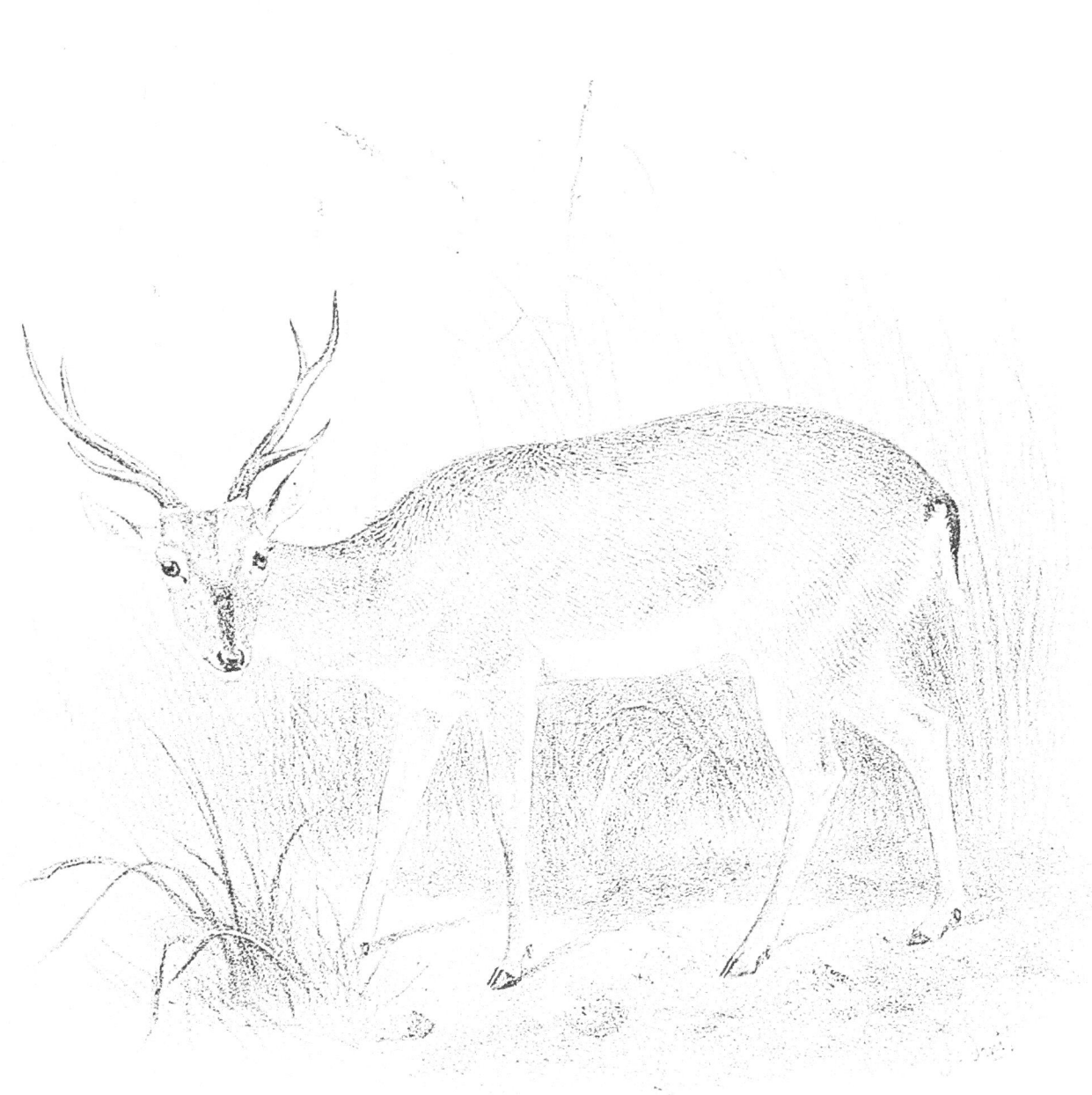

PAMPAS DEER.

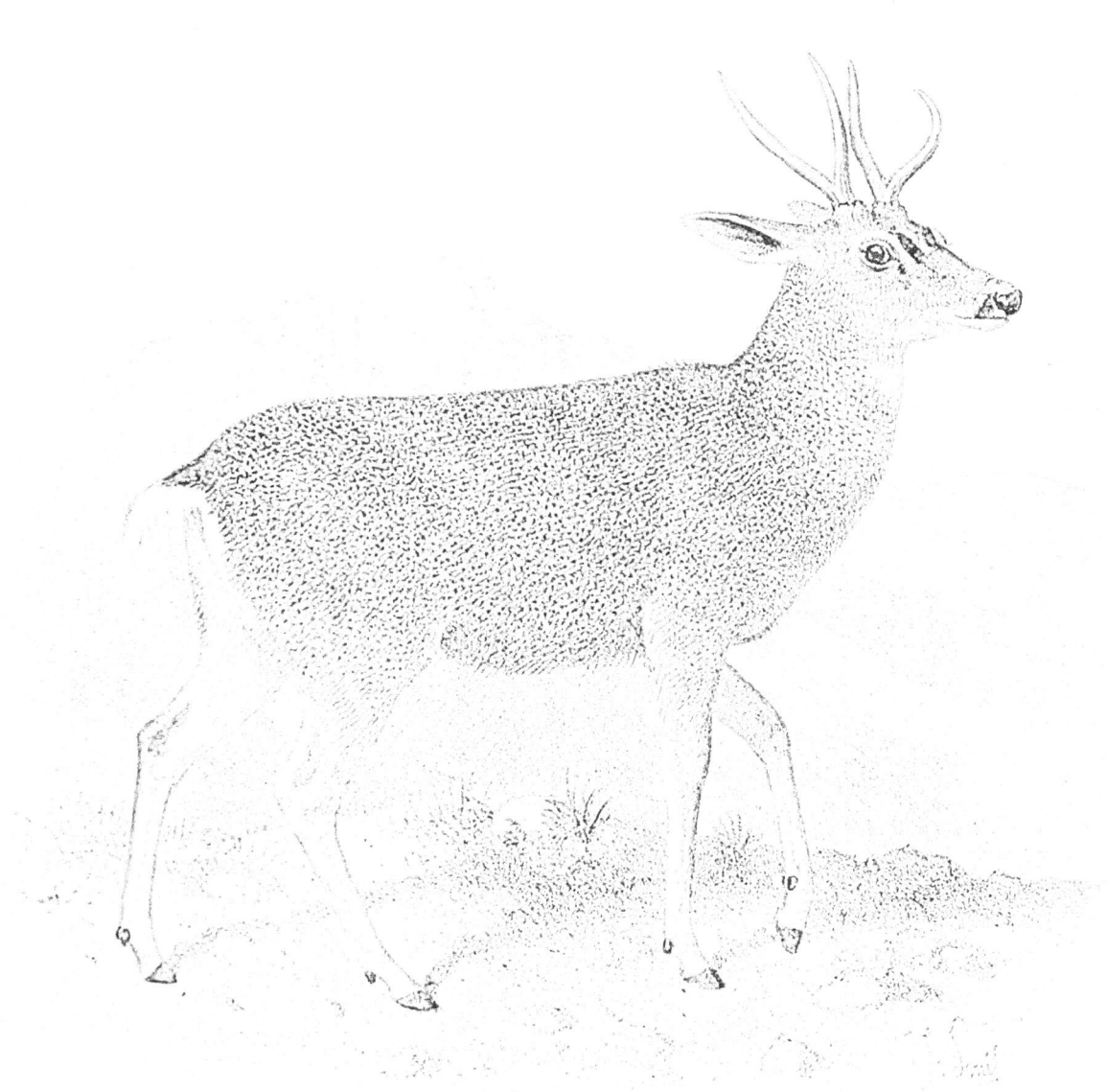

PERUVIAN GUEMAL.

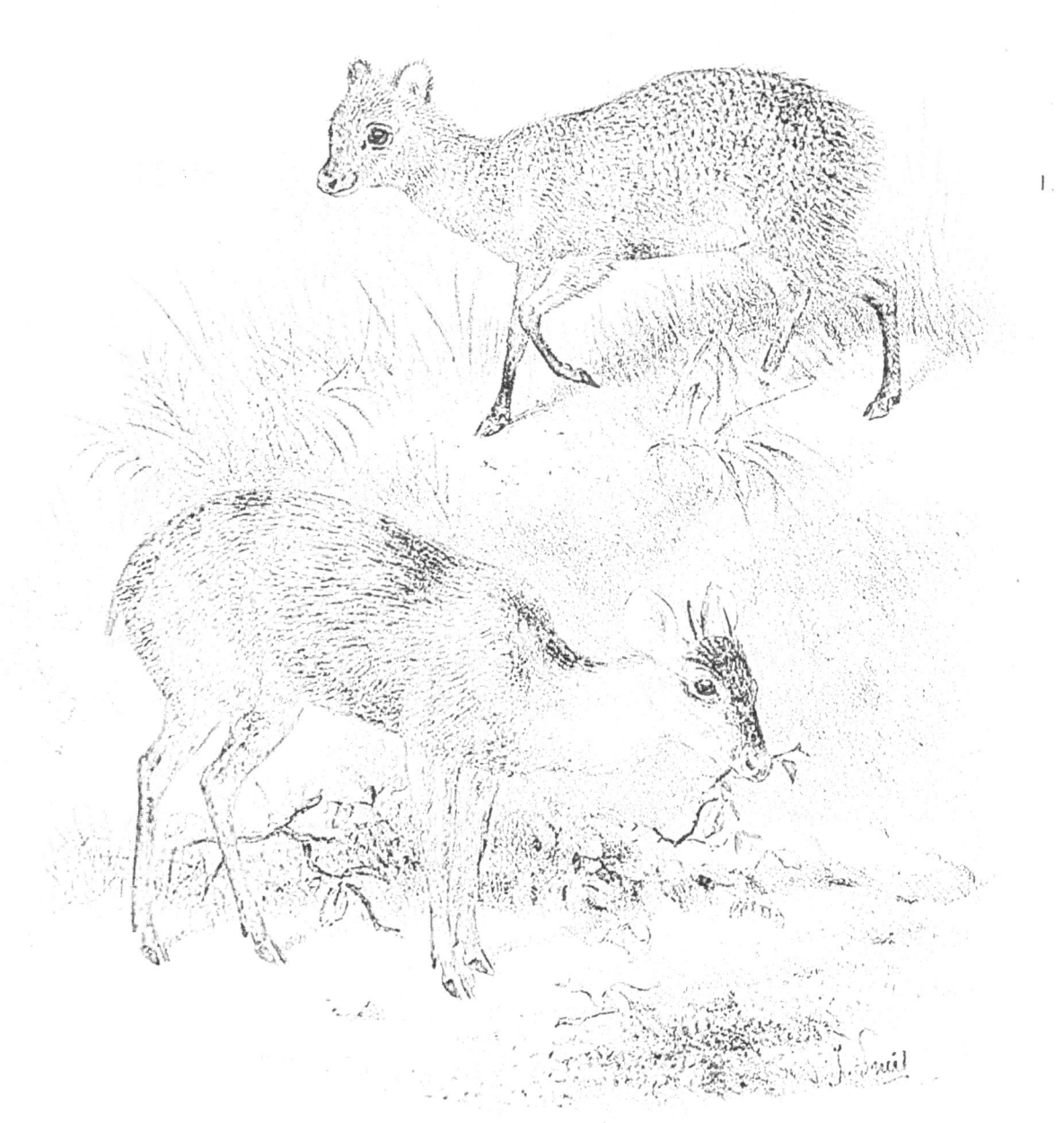

ECUADOR PUDU (1) AND CENTRAL AMERICAN BROCKET (2).

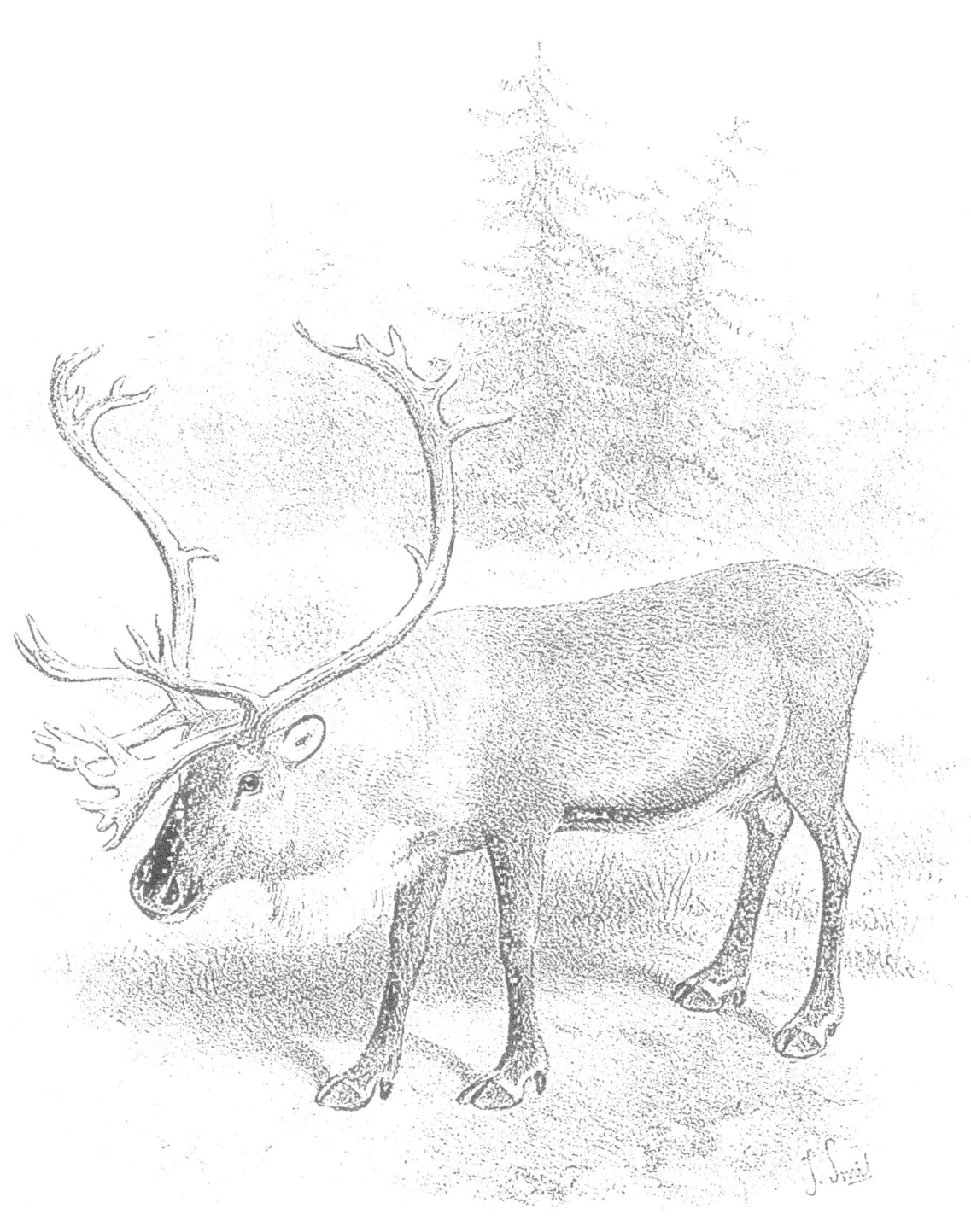

SCANDINAVIAN REINDEER.